This...
...is about life.

Book I:
Cherish Your Beginning

a collection of poems
from 1969-1973

by Randi Owens

...is about life.

Book I:
Cherish Your Beginning

*a collection of poems
from 1969 - 1973*

by: Randi Owens

By: Randi Owens

Editor: Emily Autenrieth

Illustrations: Kimberly Gallardo

Copyright ©
Printed in the U.S.A.
ISBN 978-0-9981443-0-6

First Edition 2016

For every cherished life...

Table of contents

Introduction

1969
    The Unknown Girl 2
    The Baby Sparrow 3
    Little Proper Bobby 4
    The Master Performer 5

1970
    To Burris by Burro 8
    Fuzz 9
    A Flight to Be Remembered 10
    Town Gossiper 11
    The Golden Cannon 12
    Let It Be Known 13
    A Special Joy 14
    The Month of May 15
    The Soft Magic Ball 16
    Who's Who! 17
    Central Cabarrus High 18
    Gooses and Mooses 19
    The Wee Little Ones 20
    The Jazz Band 21
    Monnie 22
    My Sister 23
    Thanksgiving 24

1971
    Halloween Is Coming 26
    Let's Join in the Groove 27

Table of contents

1971
- Sunny Benton 28
- The Lonesome Tomboy 29
- I'm The Champ 30
- Sixteen and Still Pushing 31
- Jackson 32
- As the Green Grass Grows 33
- The Mysterious Mystery 34
- Rats Are Rats 35
- Sleepyhead 36
- Somber Generation Gaps 37
- Poor Sad Cherrie 38
- My Horse Tale 39
- Gay Tucker 40
- Mr. Wensil 41
- How Can I Hold My Temper? 42
- Nobody Really Cared 43
- The Falling Leaves 44
- Typing I and Mr. James 45
- This House 46
- The Judge 47

1972
- Listen 50
- Soul People 51
- It Takes Friends 52
- The King of Nations 53
- Sweet Blonde Annie 54
- Merry Christmas 55
- A Small Poem of Wisdom 56
- I Often Wish That I Could Sing 57

Table of contents

1972

Someone Listens Every Single Day 58
Emma Fish 59
Lessons about Work 60
A Very Special Easter 61
My Heart Within 62
We've Been Missing You 63
My Dreams 64
Typing II and Mr. Harris's New Rules 65
In Hell 66
One Last Chance 67
No One Can Blow it Away 68
The Fog 69
Trouble 70
Prayer 71
Fighting 72
I Am an Outsider 73
The Onlooker 74
Mr. Barnes, Don't Retire ... Yet 75
Because 76
Jenny Harris, Happy Birthday 77
Driver's Education: Following Directions 78
While I Sat Here 79
Death Is Near 80
Life Is Dull 81

Table of contents

1973
- COURAGE 84
- Why? 85-86
- I Often Wonder 87
- Gretel at School 88
- I Made a Fool of Myself 89
- What Should I Say? 90
- Don't Monkey Around 91
- Mr. Nicey 92
- The Good Old Days 93
- The Teacher of Bethlehem 94
- Jolly Jolly 95
- Some Things Are Changeable 96
- I'm Still Looking 97
- The Alleyway 98
- A Life of Your Own 99
- A Guy Named Gary 100
- Good Ole George 101
- Togetherness 102
- A Chance 103
- Peace 104
- People Are Different 105
- Viking Team 106
- An Outstanding Personality 107
- It's That Time Again 108
- A Sudden Change in Life 109
- Drawing Designs 110
- 4-H 111
- I Thank You 112
- GTO 113
- My Living Angel 114

Introduction

I wrote the following poems over a period of five years, beginning when I was 14 and in middle school. They proved to be a valuable lifeline when I believed there were no other viable alternatives for dealing with my feelings.

Poetry can provide therapeutic relief from worries and life's excess stressors. It invites readers to incorporate their thoughts and emotions into the words, creating the opportunity for temporary breaks from everyday life encounters. Through the poems, I learned that it was okay to be upset, smile, laugh, and cry, and to simply live. We can intertwine and cross what's real with fantasy ... if only just for that moment in time. I invite you to enter the world of an adolescent woman in the early 70s and bring your thoughts and emotions with you.

1969

The Unknown Girl

I met a very nice girl in the hall on my first day of school, to my delight
I seemed to run into her every day for a while, but today she was out of sight

She was the one who took time to show me to all of my high school classes
She introduced me to the office staff as she explained hall passes

She paused to introduce herself and tell me her name before she left
I was surprised by her kindness and overtaken by the emotions I felt

No one else approached me or tried to acknowledge my head nod of "Hi"
 They looked away, snickered, said mean things, or simply walked on by

At times, I thought I saw the unknown girl in a crowd surrounded by peers
It was her kindness that helped me to accept and understand my people fears

If I should see her face-to-face again I would smile, as if meeting a long lost friend
The unknown girl crossed the color barrier to be nice when others chose to offend

The Baby Sparrow

Once I awoke from sleep
.....and looked out the window to take a peek

As I sat peeking out so soon
.....I saw a baby sparrow creeping up towards my room

He looked like he needed to be in a nest
I carefully placed him on a towel in my hope chest

The baby sparrow chirped as it sought a meal
I looked out a window but saw no mother bird still

I only had rice and chicken from the night before
The baby sparrow watched as I walked out the bedroom door

I prepared the food with care, adding milk and cream
This is how he liked it--or so it seemed

I fed my baby sparrow with this mixture every day
He grew beautiful feathers for flight and one day flew away

I miss my baby sparrow but he visits now and then
Sometimes I think I hear him chirping in the early morning

Little Proper Bobby

Little Proper Bobby was rich--and poor
When he saw money, he always wanted more

When he walked along the streets, everyone looked down
He connected with nobody as he acted like a clown

Little Proper Bobby thought he was King of them all
Until he reached the bank and found he was broke as a glass kickball

With the money he had left, he bought a grand little home
He stayed to himself because he felt he was all alone

Over time, Bobby learned that money wasn't to his heart true
And that with all of the money in the world, he still needed love too

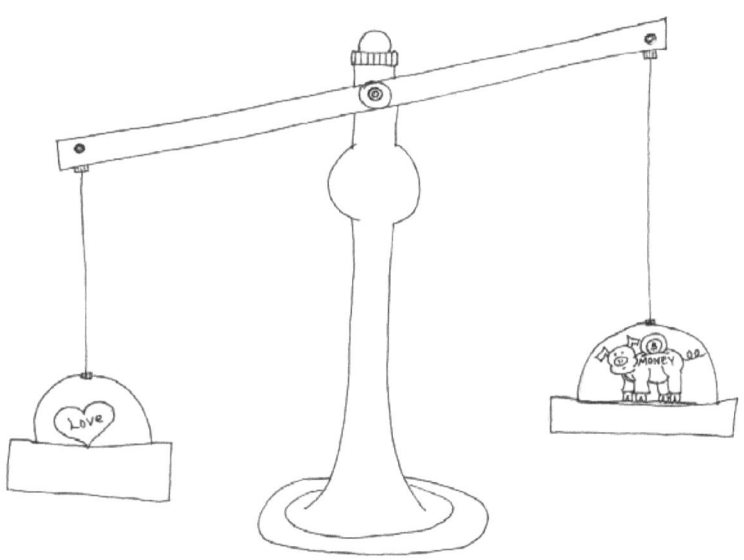

The Master Performer

Loretta is her name, and there are times when she's nice
But other times, she's mean, and you pay the price

To equal the performance of a master hand....
....She had to push herself to work like a good strong man

She worked in the forest, driving trucks and hauling wood
She made it look easy, but I knew it was hard work with all the time it took

Loretta was a master performer with a minimum education
She learned from a school of hard knocks with her sixth-grade limitations

Her life was never easy and watching her, you couldn't tell
That some people in her life went through living hell

1970

To Burris by Burro

My favorite aunt lives in Burris, and I want to visit her there
She lives near the field where every year, they have the country fair

Travel by Burro is tedious, but you get to see all the sights
My Burro has to stop several times to nibble and get a bite

It's important to pack absolute necessities and bring nothing more
I am told I may not have a chance to buy things at a store

My Burro may get me to Burris in a couple of months or so
But I'm in no hurry as long as I get to where I need to go

The old family car would be an option if I could afford the fuel
But my Burro's cheaper than the car, a horse, or my sister's mean old mule

We have a companionable trip, my Burro and I
Neither of us says very much as we wave to the occasional passerby

Riding my Burro to Burris to visit my favorite aunt in town
...gives me the idea to seek new friends until I decide to settle down

I'm not one to stay too long in one place, you see
But I'll never forget the adventure of riding my Burro cross-country

Fuzz

"What kind of name is 'Fuzz'?" I was often asked by the girls
I'd say, it's the name of a man that's going places in the world

I've been told all of my life that my name is sort of strange
It was thought up by my mom and is one I will never change

Although she is no longer alive, she had big dreams for me
I plan to make her proud and make the name Fuzz part of history

I am close to completing my education--
and look forward to a life of unknown equations

The girls will have to wait, as I plan to take life slow
I want to be a positive influence and maybe someone's hero

A Flight to Be Remembered

A flight to be remembered, is one you'll never forget
A flight to be remembered, is one racing past a jet
A flight to be remembered, is one set aside
A flight to be remembered, is one you never ride
A flight to be remembered, is one where you did not die
A flight to be remembered, is one you thought of with a sigh
A flight to be remembered, is one where you landed without a hurt
A flight to be remembered, is one where you deplaned first

Town Gossiper

Since the gossiper was out of town
The silencer was to make a sound

To his surprise, and others' too
That little silencer spoke like You Know Who

The gossiper returned looking so sad, and we all had to know:
The poor gossiper could no longer put on a gossip show

His tongue was silent, and he wouldn't speak a word
Beware, all gossipers, to think before you speak of what you've heard

The Golden Cannon

Rolling down the hill, just like Jack and Jill
Was the golden cannon of Hillbilly Hill

Everyone's deep wish was to get the cannon bold
Because of its power to fire cannonballs of gold

The way it got away from everyone, no one has yet found out
They all had their minds on gold as they sought its whereabouts

The golden cannon was really a girl, turned to a cannon by a witch in a black gown
She soon returned to her normal form and no gold was to be found

Let It Be Known

Let it be known as I describe the condition of few--
that of completeness in life, with nothing left to do--

Let it be known that we all have our parts
We'll either do them well or begin from the start

The condition of believing you have done it all
Leaves you setting yourself up for a fall

The year of 1970 has been full of lessons I've learned
On this, my birthday, let it be known that it's my turn

There are many that believe they know everything of their plight
Let it be known, this condition is temporary with an end in sight

A Special Joy

There is a special joy for you and me
Of Mommy and Daddy, and their memory

The special joy to us comes but once a year
When in the foster home there's fun, with only a few tears

Everyone's happy on this joyful day
Because of the answered prayers we each chose to say

There's a lot of happiness in our Christmas joy
On this day I'll remember my foster siblings, the girls and boys

The Month of May

The month of May can be quite gloomy
Except for the flowers that are blooming

May does not speak as loudly as other months do
but when it does, it feels like it's speaking to you

Although it is said that April showers bring May flowers and less rain
I say the tears of the April showers bring May's memories and a soft pain

The days of the month of May surrounding Mother's Day are the best
They help me recall my mother's presence, instilling peace instead of sadness

The Soft Magic Ball

The soft magic ball was in a small box
When in the daylight, you'd think it had smallpox

One day as it rolled along on the earthly ground
Out of nowhere came a furious hound

The ball rolled towards its friend in a circle of dice
Only to miss the circle and fall into some nearby ice

When it got out of the ice, it was very very cold
The once-soft ball has never again been soft enough to roll

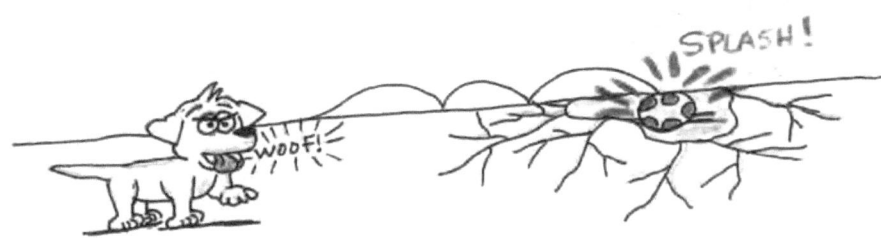

Who's Who!

Weldon was the older, but you couldn't tell them apart
Wayland was the younger, but this was just the start

Wayland wanted to work where he could eat a lot
Weldon was greedy too, and so he worked in the same spot

Weldon got B's in most of his classes
But Wayland got A's when he wore his glasses

Who's Who is the question, but that's not the worst for the twins
They often switched looks to confuse teachers and friends

Central Cabarrus High

The classes are great at Central Cabarrus and the teachers are kind
My grades from last year leave me not too far behind

Six classes I have to locate in this new High School
I have to sit and be intelligent and not look like a fool

Home Economics is great for the girls that are here
Although we have to work hard, we have nothing to fear

Math, I guess, beats all the rest because of how it's done
I often become frustrated because it is not a lot of fun

Central Cabarrus is full of prejudices and everyone has something to say
The school offers opportunity, and I refuse to just quit and go away

The sadness that I feel is not because of the color barriers that exist
Disappointment is in black peers treating me just as meanly as the whites that persist

Central Cabarrus High, no, it is not the school that is to blame
There's as many good students here as there are those seeking to earn a name

Gooses and Mooses

Gooses and Mooses all lying around
Gooses and Mooses all over the ground

Gooses and Mooses fighting up a cloud
Gooses and Mooses making noises so loud

What they were fighting over they didn't know
They just began fighting when they heard a whistle blow

One day they stopped and looked at their torn hide and feathers pulled
They left the path of fight to wash up, have a good laugh, and walk into the woods

The Wee Little Ones

There was once a wee little boy, and very wee was he
There was once a wee little girl, and very wee was she

They both went to school and had some fun at times
You could tell they weren't happy when they were always last in line

They worked really hard in school and knew what to do
They shared their belief of do unto others as you would have them do unto you

They were young and full of fun and joy
They accepted their differences from other girls and boys

They sought out other playmates with encouragement and invite
With their determination, every student was gradually drawn to their plight

No child should be left out or always placed at the back of the line
They each deserve a chance to blossom and succeed over time

The Jazz Band

Lanny was the young leader of this band
When he was around girls he acted all man

Charlie was happy as he played on the drums
Never missing a beat as he poured down his rum

Harold was laid back as he played on his guitar
Smiling with joy as he smoked on his cigar

Don played the saxophone, making soulful sounds
Tapping his feet to the beat of the rhythm he'd found

Carmen was on piano and she knew how to play
Her fingers flew across the keys as the crowd danced away

Lanny's voice always drew in the crowd as the jazz band played in the dim light
Everyone enjoyed themselves each Saturday … if only for the one night

Monnie

Monnie has soul but he was never told
If I had soul I'd really take hold

If you want soul, just get with the beat,
Shake it up baby and move those feet

You've got to have talent to be as good as Monnie ... in a way
But don't bump it because talent is not all you'll need to stay

Monnie has soul and is young, free, happy, and loves to play
Unlike the old souls suffering from a lack of joy to display

My Sister

My sister Sallie Mae is as bright as is the day
She is bright in a most unusual way

Her face is as bright as a yellow lily
But she looks just like our goat named Billy

If you think this is silly
You should see my other sister, Molly Milly!

She has long legs and a laugh that is shrilly
And she runs like our horse named Frilly

My sister, well, I guess I have more than one on display
They are both fun to be with as we each munch on our hay

Thanksgiving

On Thanksgiving Day, I'll have to eat turkey as I enjoy my meal
While I'm eating my turkey delight I'll think of the rest of my food with zeal

The first Thanksgiving, with the Indians and the Pilgrims on the Plains
Gives true meaning to this special day and what it meant to those that came

The Indians brought hope to the feast, which was fraught with wars of doom
They sought friendship with the Pilgrims as they ate by the light of the moon

There are battles and wars still being fought by many in every race
They can choose to make turkey dressing together, or throw eggs in each other's face

Let us give thanks to the Indians and the Pilgrims too
For bringing to light the evils of war and the possibilities of friendship made anew

1971

Halloween Is Coming

Halloween is coming and the children are all at play
Halloween is coming and the parents start to pray

There are visions on Halloween that are frightening and ghostly
You wear bright colors to be seen from a distance and make-up for effect up closely

If you dress up like a witch, clown or wear a mask like a fowl
You're less likely to be mistaken as searching about on the prowl

Halloween is coming and I'm looking forward to the fun and candy
Halloween is coming and it's the one time of year when we laugh unabashedly

Halloween is coming and we can dress up and look a fright
Halloween is coming and we'll have some fun tonight

Let's Join in the Groove

There was a small hut out in the sand facing towards the sun
Many times, we all went to this hut to have a little fun

Some of the group would not be with the beat of the game
While there were others I believe, that were about the same

I'd jump up and down and say out loud
"Let's join in the groove … or we can move with the crowd"

Strangely, they look mad as they move away with a sad look on their face
And since I'm new around town, I move along with their much slower pace

I didn't know I was considered an outsider, so I didn't make note of their need
For me to close my mouth and realize that they wanted me to take heed

Sunny Benton

Sunny Benton was her name and she was bright as the sun
And within her lively eyes all you could see was fun

She was nice to me and everyone else she could see
Sunny Benton was a kind spirit at heart because she felt so free

This is only one of the reasons Sunny Benton was her name
There were many other names to fill her brightness just the same

I wish I could have a heart as big as hers in life
Although Sunny Benton wouldn't be my name because I'm too full of strife

The Lonesome Tomboy

Phyl was a young missy and a tomboy too
If Phyl acted like a missy I wouldn't know what to do

One day she went to Thomasville and climbed every tree
She climbed trees like her brother and she climbed them better than me

Phyl was not a small thing but nor was she too big
When she went to market she would always dance the Jig

Of all the things she did, Phyl was still just a lonesome kid
Phyl's boyfriend's name was Sid and he didn't like anything that she did

Phyl enjoyed being a tomboy but she was still pretty sad
Especially since Sid was her boyfriend but always acted like he was her dad

I'm The Champ

I'm the champ of New Orleans
I've got a shape like a washing machine

I beat their champ and beat him clean
I buried him in a casket that really gleamed

Now that he is dead and gone
I can settle down and make my home

I can boss all of the others around
Because I'm the new champ of this old town

Sixteen and Still Pushing

Have you heard the phrase, "16 and never been kissed?"
Until you try it, you don't know what you've missed

I am sixteen and still pushing without having had a first date
Other boys talk about relationships as they say sixteen is kind of late

I am sixteen and from a family well-to-do
One day I went to a girl's house, someone I wanted to woo

I still hadn't kissed a girl but I thought she was the one to be by my side
As I looked on, I died a little and felt myself swallow my pride

A first kiss is something I believed special and looked forward to it with joy
I am sixteen and still pushing, but my girl may be learning to kiss from another boy

I believe there is still time and I will patiently wait
Other girls will come along and I look forward to kissing those dates

Jackson

I'm going to Jackson ... by train or plane
I'm going to Jackson ... from whence I came
I'm going to Jackson ... I'll pack my sack
I'm going to Jackson ... I ain't coming back
I'm going to Jackson ... Do you want to come along?
I'm going to Jackson ... back to my born home
I'm going to Jackson ... You just wait and see
I'm going to Jackson ... then I'll know I'm free
I'm going to Jackson ... where Mom and Dad once lived
I'm going to Jackson ... where my roots are still

As the Green Grass Grows

As the green grass grows high and tall it seems no one ever cares
when it comes time they'll see the grass is often better than chairs

I like the grass and the way it grows, but what I'll find nobody knows
This is the season for the snakes to be seen and into the beautiful grass they'll go

During the winter it all dies out
As during the spring it grows green and stout

Sometimes the green grass grows sparse and wild
Yet its beauty will always make me smile

The Mysterious Mystery

This tale is of the rich and the poor
Of how they felt when there was money no more

This mysterious mystery began at midnight
It was utterly dark, not a person in sight

As the church bell rang out clear and loud
Out of the dark came a mysterious crowd

I know they weren't people because they had horns
Neither were they ghost because none were born

And now the mystery that is still at hand
….Were the thieves that took all of the world's money myth or man?

Rats Are Rats

Rats are rats and that is that
... they can't be dogs, they can't be cats

One day I was playing in a field when a rat came close
I pretended it wasn't there as I backed into a post

I admit I was afraid because it was so big
It was afraid of me too as it ran towards a hole where it hid

"Rats are rats," and your fear can't change that
They won't turn into dogs or cats, they'll always remain rats

Sleepyhead

Wobbling his head back and forth, he fell asleep one day
Poor sleepyhead was late for school because he fell asleep in the hay

Sleepyhead felt tired and was very very sad
Because he missed his assignments, which made him pretty mad

"Sleepyhead," I said one day, "try harder to stay awake"
Because if you don't, think of all the low grades you will make

Sleepyhead remembered the words I placed in his head
Do not sleep in class, go home in time to do your work, and go to bed

Somber Generation Gaps

The things today that are plaguing me
are what to do if, while in the fog, I cannot see

Generation gaps I don't understand
The way people are coming, there's almost not enough land

There are generation gaps between so many on earth
It ends with dying but begins with birth

We don't really need a somber generation gap around
But how can we stop it when its ties to life abound?

We know this isn't the way it should be
Any somber generation interferes with our ability to be free

Poor Sad Cherrie

Cherrie was sad because her guy had left
She went into the kitchen and put her heart upon a shelf

If another came by, she'd act shy
If he offered her love, she'd ask why

Poor Cherrie was really out of her mind
She never again wanted to see the sunshine

Cherrie cried her heart back in again
As she went looking for another man

My Horse Tale

This is a tale that beats them all
It is a tale of Linda Tall

When she went into her stall
She'd always walk right into the wall

This is the beginning and that's not all
Linda was skinny and almost bald

Within my tale I cannot really recall
Whether this happened during summer, winter, spring, or fall

Linda wasn't allowed to run with the other mares on the farm
She was blind in one eye and there was fear that she could be harmed

Linda Tall was happy just giving the small children a ride at a slow pace
This gave her a chance to exercise and visit with the other mares in her space

My Horse Tale is a tribute to a mare that brought much joy into my lonely heart
I miss my friend, her uneven gait, sloped back, and eyes that were forever dark

Gay Tucker

"Doctor, where is my baby? I wish to see her now, please"
"Nurse, bring in the Tucker baby, the one with the ink still on her feet"

"Did you say my baby is sick? I can't tell"
"She is smiling and looks happy and well"

"She is a little thin, and maybe a tad bit pale"
"I just want to hold her and love on her for a spell"

"She's not ill, Ms. Tucker, but needs to return to the nursery soon"
"She's so soft, cuddly, and cute … can she stay a little longer in my room?"

"Mr. Tucker, have you chosen your baby's name?"
"I'll let my wife do it, thank you just the same"

"Ms. Tucker, what would you like her to be called?"
"She is so wide awake and happy, so the name Gay or nothing at all"

Mr. Wensil

I feel bored sitting in homeroom class, just listening to what others say
My school work is complete, the bell has yet to ring, and I'm ready to start my day

Mr. Wensil is talking and I think I missed what he said
I hope it wasn't important because I had other thoughts in my head

His assignments are not hard, and he's a good teacher too
He's helpful, answering questions as he makes sure you know what to do

We are located outside of the main school in a big trailer off to the side
Sometimes it's difficult to get there on time because the path isn't very wide

Mr. Wensil looks like he really enjoys teaching the class as he draws us in
I realize I feel relaxed as I leave his classroom, ready for my day to begin

How Can I Hold My Temper?

How can I hold my temper when I get upset and mad?
I always try to act as though I am happy and glad

I stuff away my feelings as though everything is alright
The pressure only builds until I get into a big wordy fight

I am afraid that someday I'm going to get upset and really blow my top
… that there's going to be so much steam, it will be difficult to stop

I don't like it when I get mad or overly upset
I'd rather do something good, like work on goals to be met

When I get mad and hurt others' feelings, I feel pretty small
I'm learning to control my temper so that I can stand tall

How can I hold my temper and not hurt the ones I love at heart?
I've decided to take a timeout, cool down, and talk to them about my part

Nobody Really Cared

Nobody really cared, even when they say they love you so
If they never hold you or listen to you, how do you really know

How do I know when I am having fun
If when someone starts to yell, I just want to run

Nobody really cared when I cut my wrist on the glass I'd found
They told me I couldn't see a doctor as I watched my blood soak into the ground

I remember running away so that I wouldn't be beaten when I got home
Nobody really cared I thought, as I listened to the lady talk to them on the phone

Why do I fight so hard when things just remain the same
Nobody really cared, do they even know my name?

When I was tripped at school, hurt my head, and had a nose bleed
Nobody really cared that I was made to walk home in the heat

I remember feeling sick and throwing up all the while
But nobody really cared....I was just a foster child

The Falling Leaves

The fallen leaves that have drifted to the ground for so long
Have finally landed to stay in their predestined home

Some are happy and glad to have finally landed
While others are sad because they'll be trampled upon by man

They do not care for such a sight during their decline
As they drift past the changes to nature's annual gift of time

The leaves are falling down to earth and man will burn some to crust
They are still in our care as we cherish them even as they turn to dust

The Spring season will come, filled with fresh blooming plants and trees
The process will begin anew bringing new birth from precious seeds

Typing I and Mr. James

Well, class, now that we're back from our short vacation ...
We'll begin where we stopped: the part about calls made station to station

We've learned that this is our cheapest means of telephone communication ...
This saves time and money, whether talking to friends or making reservations

According to my thoughts about this book's publication ...
Most of the titles in it, place great emphasis on its dedication

The book falls short of my teaching expectations ...
Therefore, it's up to me to give you material to encourage your participation

However, before you leave this course and prior to your graduation ...
I'm going to teach you my method of lifelong typing education

This House

This house is the loneliest house in town
No one is stirring; there is not even a sound

Up the streets and down there's nobody around
This house is the loneliest house I've ever found

Not a word spoken, not even in distress
There is only silence and a distant quietness

If you were to see such a house and ask to come in
You'd know it isn't my house, because my house is noisy and always has been

The Judge

Here comes the judge with the jury close behind
Here comes the judge as the courtroom stands and the gavel hits the pine

As the witness gets on the stand and the jury sits down
Those that are guilty think of packing their bags to leave town

When the judge begins to rise because the case is complete
When the jury is excused, the verdict of guilty peaks your curiosity

Stay on the good side of the law so you'll not come before a judge accused of a crime
Accept your need for responsibility too self and by extension, to mankind

1972

Listen

Listen to the heavenly horn so high
And hear the Angels singing in the sky

They are singing "do not cry;
"There will come a day when you will all die"

Listen to the holy bells ringing with the heavenly tide
They are ringing in harmony as they sway side to side

Listen to the Holy words these precious sounds have to tell
Accept all of humanity as your spirit hums to the sound of heavenly bells

Soul People

Soul people are not limited in color as they move around in a whirl
The way they fuss and fight you wouldn't think they were boy or girl

I wish someday this all would stop, before it is too late
The souls of people are separate, unique, special, and not up for debate

I am hopeful that someday everyone will stop and settle down
As they realize we all need each other in order to stay around

Although I can never do for others what they must do for themselves with might
I find myself mentally pushing them along and encouraging them in their plight

The souls of people are fraught with personal choice
We can remain silent and watch or we can give it freedom and voice

It Takes Friends

It takes friends to be happy and content throughout the day
Because without them, in your life satisfaction is difficult to display

It takes friends when you have sad thoughts within your head
Some thoughts are there because of the cruel things that are said

Make-believe friends are hurtful, their painful intent hard to see
They stab your back as they smile and falsely act friendly

If I had true friends, my life hardships would hardly be of note
I'm sad almost every day; I think of what it feels like to walk into the lake and float

It takes friends to help you realize how temporary each moment in life can be
It takes friends to help you conquer your feelings of sadness and being lonely

The King of Nations

The king of the nations was greatly known for his pride
One day he went into another kingdom and stole that king's bride

He took her far into the hills and left her there to cry
Since she was alone night and day she wished that she could die

Although the king went to see her secretly, he wasn't aware of his plight
She felt no better because she knew she did not belong to him by right

The king's wife heard of her husband's romance and threatened his life
She was the true ruler in the kingdom, having his head removed with his knife

The king's wife was not very sad for what she had just done in grief
She had the queen of the other nation's head cut off to give her more relief

Sweet Blonde Annie

Sweet Blonde Annie was as sweet as could be
But when she got mad she took it all out on me

Sweet Blonde Annie was small and stout
When she felt sad, all she'd do was pout

This wasn't very good for her given name
She thought being a blonde was part of a game

When Sweet Blonde Annie was old enough to marry a man
She changed her name to plain ole Ann!

Merry Christmas

Merry Christmas to everyone as you keep peace within your hearts
May the end of the season bring a joyful new year with fresh starts

Try not to be sad on such a lovely Christmas day
Have a jolly good time as you watch the children play

Set aside some time to sing joyously and to pray
Merry Merry Christmas to you all in every way

If you are among those with enough to share
Praise God for your willingness to continue to care

A Small Poem of Wisdom

Here is a poem that has no end
… of how you'll be if you commit a sin
… you'll feel blind with sight and no real friends

You will listen to what you want to hear, knowing it is not quite right
… the blinding image of yourself moves past as you've almost lost your sight
… you are not out of the darkness, but still looking forward to the light

Everything you touch sets your nerve endings on fire
… you do very little and yet you easily tire
… you view life as a loss and your future at times, looks dire

As you open your mouth you can't say a word
… no one is listening, you can't be heard
… your heart slows to a flitter like the wings of a small bird

Give back what was never yours to receive
… seek to free yourself from the tethers of those you deceive
… release the burdens of the sins you choose to perceive

I Often Wish That I Could Sing

I often wish that I could sing and that I had a beautiful voice
Instead I enjoy writing as my favorite pastime choice

I often wish that I could sing, but I like listening to those that can carry a tune
It's because of their voices that I've learned to appreciate my talent so soon

I often wish that I could sing, and be gracious in the fame
I know that if I were to sing there would be humiliation and shame

I often wish that I could sing … perhaps one of my poems could be a song
There has to be a beautiful voice to match my thoughts that are so loud and strong

I often wish that I could sing, but nobody would listen, I confess
I'll leave the singing to the gifted voices that can do it the best

Someone Listens Every Single Day

Someone listens every single day but they don't always hear what you have to say
There are times when you try to be serious and they want to have fun and play

Everyone's life has a story to tell with the hurts, pains, and heartaches
The right person at the right time isn't always possible without making mistakes

Someone listens every single day because they want to reach out and offer hope
There are others that listen because they need to gossip in order to cope

Someone listens every single day and you never know what they will learn
Be careful of what you say because there are ears at every turn

Someone listens every single day many with problems like you and me
The inner strength we each have reinforces who we'd like to be

Remember to listen carefully to what is being said
They may be taking time to talk to you to plant seeds of wisdom in your head

Emma Fish

"Emma Fish, set my dish, and remember ... you're my maid
Tough on you for not wanting to, because I'm the one to make sure you get paid"

Although Emma was not my maid, in fact, as she told me with a shout
It really annoyed me and made me mad when she would begin to pout

Emma was pretty big for her humble self, often taking up a lot of space
When she sat on occasion for tea, she'd choose the most comfortable seat
   in the place

Emma was kind to me and accepted all of my faults and limitations
It was because of Emma that I learned to accept myself and my situation

Because I could not walk without help, I often took her kindness for granted
As we grew older and apart, I used as a resource the many seeds she had planted

Emma moved on, going to college and having a family of her own
I tracked her down and made plans to visit--even though I'd never flown

As I hobbled forward with my daughter by my side at the end of my flight
I smiled with joy as my best friend came into sight

We hugged and cried and laughed out loud as we talked about the past
Our daughters quietly watched as we discussed hopes and dreams
   that came true at last

Lessons about Work

The boss came and my work was not done
The first thing I thought was, "I really want to run"

Mr. Clark was not mean, I just didn't want to do my part
And when he asked why, I lied and said it was my heart

That lie stayed on my mind as I began to work without a word
One day Mr. Clark commented and I felt good about what I'd overheard

I was given a raise in pay for doing my share and more
It made a difference when I began to pull my weight in such a small store

The load proved balanced and fair when helping to build relationships rather than destroy
I thank Mr. Clark for lessons on working hard and accepted the challenge to remain employed

A Very Special Easter

This Easter is one we will not forget
because it is not like all the rest

It is different in many ways, the same as are we
... Our race celebrates it as do the other races I see

On Easter Sunday do we think of our Christ and hold him close
... or is he merely stuffed away as in our Sunday attire we boast?

Does he not want us to be equal regardless of the race
... so why are we so set against acceptance of each other's face?

I can't speak for another's mind
... but I can see what to some remains so blind

When someone is happy, full of joy and glad
... something happens along to make them sad

Let us enjoy this Easter and remember our father in Christ
... who gave his only son that he might restore to us Life

My Heart Within

My heart within I cannot describe
... The love I feel because I'm happy you're well and alive

If ever you need me, you know where I am
... you know I'll come running to save my sweet lamb

Pity for some I have within my heart so true
... love I have also, but for one person or maybe two

So, let no one cause us to fail in our journey for peace
... Let's show the world our hearts proving that the love within will never cease

We've Been Missing You

You've been gone for a long, long time and we miss you so
When will you come back to us? We really want to know

You see, you are our father and living far away
We seldom see you except for the occasional stay

We've been missing you, dear ole dad, since you've been gone
I think we're going to need you back because we're sad and all alone

Well, you seem to be leaving us yet again, our ever absent dad
Only this time we're happy, because we realize when you're here,
    you make us feel sad

My Dreams

I have dreams ... good and bad, of times young and old
one night I had a special dream about the winter, when it was very cold

I've heard at times of some dreams that come close to true
because my dream was just what I wanted, it won't come true, I assure you

A dream come true is something you can call your own, like your toy
It is something I consider to be my personal joy

My dream I will not mention or share, although it is really fun to have at heart
I'll keep it to myself because it could give me a fresh start

I think I may miss having my dreams after I'm put to rest someday
But I know I will hold true to my dreams because mine they will always stay

Typing II and Mr. Harris's New Rules

Now class, let's get settled down
Carol Lean, will you stop looking around

Do the conditional practice on page 309
You have only 20 minutes and you're already behind

... Stop just a moment, I have something to say
Cut off the typewriters and put your hands away

Some of you will pass my Typing II class
It will be because you listened and caught on fast

As for those that may fail under my supervision
All I can say is that it is your decision

O.K., you may go back to completing the assignment
There goes the bell ... but don't you feel our time was well spent?

My name is Mr. Harris, as if you don't already know
And, if you don't like my rules ... then you are free to go

In Hell ...

Open the door and step right in--
Don't be afraid, we're all your friends

Step over there and ring that damn bell,
now you know you're in hell

You've been on earth, having so much fun
...and now it's time to face up to all of your harm

You know it's too late to ever turn back
...so you'd better learn your new life, fact by fact

Before you awake, follow every single step
...and when you finally die, "Don't seek my help!"
(Welcome to Hell---the Devil is back!!!)

One Last Chance

I said I wouldn't give up and I promised I would try
My poetry is my life, which means much to me, and isn't a lie

There was one last chance for me to fully make the scene
But everyone was planning and could not help me with my scheme

I said I wouldn't give up my one last chance, I know
But if my poetry isn't noticed soon, where will my life go?

Will they burn my diary all written in my poems to see
… or will they help to make my last chance a joyful memory?

I have no answer to my questions, but want the poems to be shown
I want to share my poetry and am determined to make my poems known

I won't do anything drastic to prove my poetry has something to say
But neither will I allow my last chance in life to simply wither away

No One Can Blow it Away

I once heard of a land with everlasting life--
I often wonder if it's as easily destroyed as a spirit without fight

There aren't many people going to this lively land
They have all distanced themselves rather than attempt to understand

This life isn't to be blown away in one whiff
There has to be enough fight within if you're to reach its lift

The everlasting life that I am speaking of
Is one filled with joy and everlasting love

It will always be here because no one can blow it away
I believe everlasting love, joy, and a wholesome life are ours to choose to stay

The Fog

Have you ever been to London to just wander in the fog of dull light?
Or to a place where you couldn't tell if you could see or were without sight?

Have you ever seen fog so thick that you bump into people before you see them?
Have you driven in fog with lights on bright and yet they look to be dim?

Has your car ever hit a bridge in the fog near a ranch
... as you try to drive in the direction of "one last chance"?

If you have done any of these things in the fog, I say
Don't fret ... the fog is just as thick near the bay

There's no fog that is all fun where you just want to sit and stare
Have you ever seen a fog where there is none other to compare?

Trouble

There is trouble everywhere I go
There is trouble and nobody wants to know
There is trouble and I have to lie low

I don't want any trouble but it seems to come my way
Once I went on a visit and had to stay all day
Because some people there had a whole lot to say

I'm pretty big and slow to move around
I'm heavy on my feet and make a lot of sounds
I don't want to have any trouble with anyone in town

Prayer

Don't walk the streets of the heavenly land
without the good Lord's guiding hand

If, while walking the golden streets, you feel the need to pray
Don't be surprised if God is there showing you the way

Don't give up until you're in the Holy Land
Now that you're here, you can speak to the Father--he'll understand

Fighting

I hate to fight because I'm not very brave
If things keep going the way they are, I'll soon be in my grave

I do some fighting, but it's mostly at school
When I have to defend myself from those I know are acting like fools

Fighting is not good for you and it can hurt pretty bad
But if I don't fight with all my might, at home I'll face my angry dad

He thinks that I am a "fraidy cat" without any backbone
He makes me wear boxing gloves to box with him when we are home alone

No, I don't like to fight, but going home a loser I can't risk
So take off your coat and gloves and put up your fists

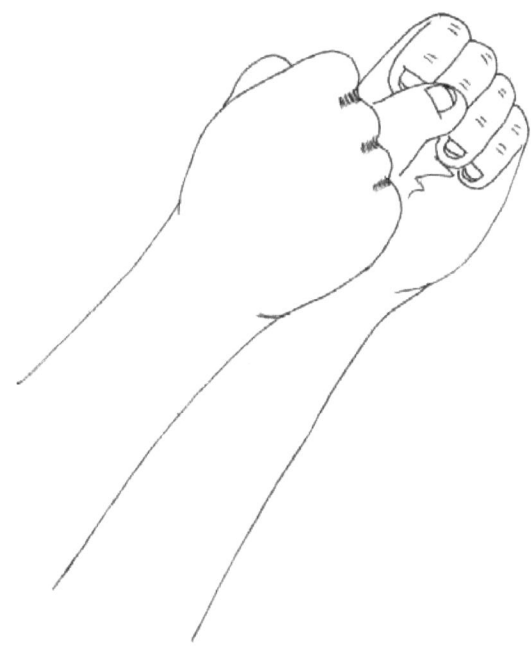

I Am an Outsider

I am an outsider, and outside I will always be
Unless I can get inside and find a friend for me

I walked around the friendship gate trying to get in
Because when I was outside, I thought I saw the eyes of a friend

I felt so down and sad as away went the sun
I went into the shade of a tree and watched everyone

I am an outsider who can't get in the friendship gate
As long as I am an outsider, I'll always be in this state

I am still an outsider, why won't you help me to get in?
I am an outsider, but I want and need a few good friends

The Onlooker

Standing at a window, looking into everyone's eyes
was an onlooker trying to find a way to die

No one quite understood the wistful look in his eyes so brown
Those gathered around could only recall him smiling and seldom wearing a frown

He was a gentle giant of great height all through school
When he graduated, many saw him about acting rather cool

He'd often back away from everyone as if he were in fright
It was difficult to understand him, but many mourned when he took his life.

Mr. Barnes, Don't Retire ... Yet

Mr. Barnes, I hear that you are going to retire from our school so young
I haven't met you face to face but I've heard much of the good things you've done

We need someone to run our school the way that only you can
Many of the students seem to believe that you are the right man

You've gotten Central up and running smoothly, never letting us down
Mr. Barnes you are the kind of person that Central really needs around

If you retire, where would we be, Central Cabarrus High School so great?
We could end up being the only school that's young and yet out of date

So, Mr. Barnes, in writing this poem, to you I'll say I am proud
and I appreciate all you do ... this is my way of speaking out loud

Because ...

Because the weather has changed, you feel sad
Because you hurt, you want everyone to feel bad

Because your heart has been broken, you have nothing to say
Because you were sent to your room, it's where you want to stay

Because you forgot what it was like to not tell a lie
Because telling the truth and not getting your way made you cry

Because you feel that you are the only one hurt, you don't even try
Because when you throw things and shut everyone out, you wonder why

Because you think the whole world has let you down
Because you think this justifies letting everyone know that you were once around
(suicide!)

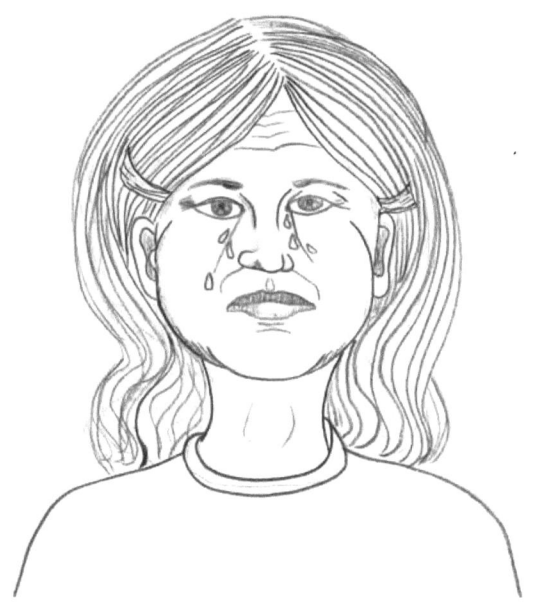

Jenny Harris, Happy Birthday

Jenny, you're the greatest, and always on my mind
Without you being near me, I would have little need for the sun to shine

Your happy smile and your lively speech are all saying one thing
That my love for your tenderness still makes my heart sing

We're getting up in years, you and I
… and our feelings for each other have yet to wither or die

I have so much more to say, Sweet Jenny, on your special day
But most of all, I want to wish you a very "Happy Birthday"

Driver's Education: Following Directions

On following directions, I think I will give you a test
I'll try to make it easy, so try to do your very best

I don't know where to start, so tell me where you are
I'll follow your directions and hope I'm not that far

I've returned to the corner where I was from the start of the drive
Maybe I miswrote the directions and have to delay when I arrive

My best notes to the test of the directions are on the very first page
Don't give up on me, please; I'm only sixteen years of age

I learned a lot in drivers' education about following directions and such
I was taught not to speed ... and a $96 ticket is a bit much

The instructor frowns at the stops I passed, more like "roll and go"
I made a few changes to my driving privilege as I practiced driving slow

Because I followed directions, I finally passed my test
It is what I need during my travels more than all the rest

I missed only one day of driver's education class
... it was the one about making sure the car has gas

While I Sat Here

While I sat here wondering why I haven't run away
The answer came to me of why I have to stay

When I first set here, I felt sad and all alone
I began to wonder about what I had done

I thought of my future and the good I wanted to do
I knew, if I ran now, no one would help me make it through

This is no way for me to want to begin
There is hope for moving forward no matter where I've been

Things haven't changed--they are as they were before
I still feel sad, but I am alone no more

I feel much better now that the weight is lifted from my chest
While I sat here wishing for more I learned to accept less

Death Is Near

Your eyes are getting weaker every day by the hour
When you wake, you find that you have little staying power

You feel strange as you move along at a slower pace
You've been given a chance to speak without haste

People are talking to each other while they are near your bed
"Death is nearer to this child than to others I know of that are already dead"

You are placed in something dark and a preacher reads from a scroll
He is saying to the people, "This child isn't very old"

Death is near and you feel it in your very soul
Your fingers are stiff and you feel so cold

You look up and see a bright light and hope you are in a heavenly land
Death is near and calling your name as he puts an end to your life plans

Life Is Dull

My life is so dull, I find it hard to get through the day
My heart is lonely and no longer wishes to stay

My dates are odd and mostly out of style
They say I'm unusual and that I never smile

My life is so dull until it makes me feel sick
I manage to get through, but it's never quick

Are you aware of how dull life can be?
When there is nothing for you to do, especially

It is difficult when life has little to offer by way of excitement
I want to have so much more than a dull life where I just vent

1973

COURAGE

It's going to take courage not to cry
It'll even take courage not to tell a lie

It's going to take courage when you're called out of your name
It's going to be really sad when you're put to shame

Though you cry to comfort the sorrow
You know it won't help because the same thing will happen again tomorrow

Use your courage to stand out from the crowd and let them know you are there
When you're spoken of in shame, don't think of when it came or from where

Allow your inner strength to shine through as you hold your head high
It takes more courage to face your troubles than it does to give in and die

Why?

Why should I live while others die?
Why should I moan while others cry?

Why should the world be full of hope
... if we will not with our problems cope?

Why do we say things about the past?
Why think of first place when you're always in last?

Why is being prejudiced ever on our minds?
Why wasn't it extinguished when it began the first time?

Why have we given up on things that are good?
Why do we labor to remain apart instead of unite in brotherhood?

Why do we falter and our strength not rebuild?
Why must we go through life with our needs unfulfilled?

Why do we lie about things that are small?
Why must we ponder our minds until we encounter a blank wall?

I often wonder how it would feel to be happy every day
... to sit among friends and listen to what everyone has to say

Why do we question the arts and creations of the world?
Why must the oyster suffer in order to create the pearl?

Why did God create us without hesitation or pause?
Why does he accept each of our individual perfections as well as our flaws?

(continued...)

(Why?)

Why is it so easy to forget the feelings of each other?
Why do we not accept that we are all sisters and brothers?

Why do we use and abuse the people we profess to love the best?
Why do we deny what is already too often stressed?

Why is it so hard to say "I want someone to care?"
Why are we always absent when we know we should be there?

Why do we often not do that which we are destined to do?
Why must we choose to live a life opposite of that which God intended us too?

I Often Wonder

I often wonder what it's like to be noticed and recognized
… to have others call you over and have conversation be the only prize

I often wonder what others would do
… if while in a crowd, I panicked and lost my cool

I often wonder if there is anyone willing to defend
… and acknowledge me as a worthy friend

I often wonder about what others may think of me and if it's really fair
… to judge me by how I look, what I wear, and if I have good hair

I often think of the one thing I dare not speak of
… as I often wonder why I have yet to feel loved

I often watch and wonder as people go places and yet go nowhere
… as I sit and wonder why I find myself unfocused as I stare

I often wonder about the many lives I wish I could have lived
… where I had little to offer to a world with so much to give

Gretel at School

Gretel is happy with her surroundings at school
She can be mean and vicious with her constant drool

Gretel wasn't a favorite of the teachers present at school late into the night
If they tried to pet her, she sometimes acted like she wanted to bite

Mr. Harwood is the only one she seems to obediently mind
He appears to be the only one to make her cold eyes shine

Once he whistles and calls out her name,
Gretel runs to find her ball because she knows it's time for a game

When Gretel is happy, her gratitude she will show
Mr. Harwood is pleased with the knowledge he has taught her to know

Gretel likes guarding the school at night with a job that earns her treats
She protects the property from vandalism and from would-be thieves

I Made a Fool of Myself

I feel like I made a fool of myself, as bad as it gets
As I stood to present my paper and I began to sweat

I could hear laughter in the back of the room
My fast-beating heart made me feel like I wanted to swoon

I feel I made a fool of myself as my ears closed down
I didn't make eye contact with anyone as I looked around

My teacher gave me fewer points than I thought I had
She said I was nervous and it interfered pretty bad

I finished my paper presentation and went to sit in my chair
I sat with my head held high as I wished myself away from there

What Should I Say?

Just this morning, I was sitting near a boy in class
He didn't stop pestering me until class ended at last

I was about to say something to him but then I began to think
Why would he say those things to me, like "you're ugly and you stink"?

I decided to ignore his words and focus on my studies
It wasn't worth the effort to respond as he laughed with his buddies

What should I say to someone who finds joy in others' misery?
He may be bored with sitting, but I'm the target of his unanswered queries

There's always a choice to make in this and similar situations if I stay
I can stand and fight with words or teach by walking away

Don't Monkey Around

One day while walking past a group of teens
I listened as they made rude gestures and said mean things

One called me a monkey in a baseball suit
I simply smiled and thought to myself, "My suit is sort of cute"

If you want to be heard and understood for what you believe
Don't monkey around! Educate others about what you hope to achieve

Teach by your example of how to treat others right
Don't monkey around or be pulled into a fight

I remind myself that I have been called much worse
Being called a monkey in a suit doesn't really hurt

The words are meant to make me feel less than smart
If I don't respond in kind, then they haven't touched my heart

Mr. Nicey

Mr. Nicey wasn't his real name, but he loved it just the same
It was important that everyone knew he cared about their attendance to the games

Jimmy was nice to people who were just passing by
Even those who said mean things and told him ugly lies

Jimmy was very special and most spoke to him with respect
His never-ending bright smile could never let you forget

Jimmy had Down's Syndrome, and he had much to offer those who knew so much
For through his kindness came wisdom and a well remembered gentle touch

To many people, Jimmy was a nice guy who was rapidly growing old
Jimmy gave fair and equal treatment, even to those giving him a shoulder so cold

We miss you Jimmy, the games are not the same
We often think of you, using Mr. Nicey as your name

The Good Old Days

In the good old days, when your parents felt that you weren't good enough
You were often punished or beaten if they believed it necessary to call your bluff

You looked forward to dating and for an opportunity to leave home
You'd pray for an excuse to bypass the curfew rather than walk through the door alone

Waiting behind the door was someone with a broom stick, belt, or switch from a tree
Later, you'd lie in bed thinking the bruises were worth the few hours to be free

Getting caught in the crossfire was not very wise back then
There was no one to save you and no one on whom you could depend

There was no room for conversation and you were warned to obey the rules
You were told to not get pregnant, sleep around, or hang out with fools

The good ole days were lacking in love, understanding, and a gentle touch
Within the home where I dwelled, a simple act of kindness cost too much

It was better to remain invisible than to be heard or seen
In the good ole days, I chose to be kind instead of being mean

The good ole days weren't as good as they were made out to be
I learned that to be silent was my very best quality

The Teacher of Bethlehem

Many people and countries have teachers but not the one I speak of
Because he spoke to his students with a voice full of acceptance and love

His name I'll not mention because it need not be
When you meet a man of such goodness you'll know of his great ability

There were many people in Bethlehem that were sick and seeking his care
There were many times when he'd stop to help as others looked on in prayer

It was as though he were on a mission and though his path was not straight
He moved with a passion that spoke of someone that was never too late

He often had a look of sadness when seeing those feeling lost and ready to die
If he could do anything to ease their pain he did so rather than walk on by

When he entered Bethlehem as he did in many cities before with trust
He never doubted his mission as he taught the lessons he knew he must

Jolly Jolly

It's time to say goodbye, once again, to the end of another school year
I'll miss all of my teachers, but as for the schoolwork, I'll not shed a tear

Jolly Jolly, I would say
Home Ec's over for good this May

I'd laugh with happiness and shout with glee
Because there is no more Math for me

With an opportunity for college should I succeed
Looking forward to helping others during their time of need

Jolly Jolly, if everything goes right and I graduate
When I pass all of my classes I'll follow the path of my fate

Some Things Are Changeable

You've argued, fussed and cursed through your life astray
Now that it's nearly over, you wish to change while you lay

Some things are changeable and some people are too
I doubt if any change will ever come over you

You get mad at anything, so mad you want to cry
Someday soon, you know you're going to die

You changed your walk, your talk, your hair color and shade
But have the changes needed most been made?

Sure, some things are changeable, but you've doomed your soul to hell
And unless you make lasting changes, your short-time life will fail

I'm Still Looking

I lost my job today because I brought my band in too play
The boss gave me that look and that was all he had to say

I took my band, instruments and all
I began my search as I waited for that one phone call

We played at weddings of young married couples
We played at nightclubs for years as we struggled

I never gave up and I still have heart
I'm still looking for a chance and a fresh start

I sort of drifted along hoping for my talent to be found
I'm still looking for a life where I share music remembered for its words and sound

The Alleyway

The wind is blowing softly and the day is quite bright
There are many paths to choose from, but I'm sure this one is right

There is a light on just past the alleyway, one that burns low
There is a tall man blocking the path to which I'm about to go

He speaks not a word, but opens a golden gate
I walk through the doors of heaven and I know I'm not too late

The angels are all singing and everyone looks like they are in place
I can't tell you what their names are because I can see no one's face

The alleyway was my destiny and so it was what I found as I went inside
That made my heart jump with joy as the golden gates were opened wide

A Life of Your Own

There's something in this world's atmosphere that hurts
I look at the people around me and I only feel worse

Some are crippled, others deaf, mute, or blind
Some move slowly in circles as though going out of their minds

I've learned to live a life of my own
I have to forget others' troubles as I stand alone

Perhaps you aren't finished with life because it can't be thrown away
It's one of the many gifts from God which allows you to choose to stay

I know you think of the poor and others you cannot help to get about
Maybe they're wealthier than you, because they know what it's like to be left without

A life of your own is well worthwhile
Think of it and treat it as if it were an only child (Cherish it!)

Let the Work of your hands Cherish and Nurture Life of your own

A Guy Named Gary

This poem is a special one, at least it is to me
You may not understand it, but there's a difference in everyone we see

Gary is very pleasant and a really nice guy
He has a sweet personality and a look that reveals he's also shy

In a way he reminds me of my only brother
Always quietly protective of everyone as we look out for one another

Most of the guys in Gary's group are judged by their fast pace
I choose to look closely at Gary's treatment of others rather than his handsome face

He has what the pretty girls want in a guy, including his beautiful car
I guess I am a little odd, because I want to see people as they truly are

There are many Garys in the world of today
Some are easier to encounter, while others go on their way

Gary died at a young age in a car crash, leaving many grieving his loss of life behind
Although he's no longer with us, he holds a special place in the hearts of those
    that knew him to be kind

Good Ole George

We can always remember my friend George Washington if we really try
He was the first president and is said to have never told a lie

He led our men into battle where we lost many of our kin
He sought to preserve life, but the losses did not justify the win

Good ole George was never really old and gray
Because he spent hours preparing his powdered wig to help it stay in place

I remember how hard it was for him at times to hold onto his pants
He'd sometimes look as though he was doing a gypsy dance

George was well known the greater part of his adult life
But once he'd fallen, it was discovered that his true fame resulted from efforts
    of his soft spoken wife

Togetherness

Will this world of togetherness overlook itself as it goes down
Will we ever take time from fighting to embrace the love to be found

There were days when we could not bear to hear the words of pending peace
And yet in this time of brotherhood, the word seems never to cease

We often hear it said, "We've come a long way"
If together we stand, we strengthen those words as we move forward day to day

Our love for our country, for the happiness of our friends
Should never waver, but instead last until the end

Should we ever falter with our peace and truthfulness
Can we ever say again that we've continued to do our best?

If once brotherhood is joined hand-in-hand
Will you with me believe in the God that created man?

A Chance

How I've waited for this chance to let my feelings all come out
To let you know what I feel life is all about

You sit and watch your students come and go
But I'm the type of kid you'll always know

You may not remember my name but that's no disgrace
Because I'm quite sure you'll not forget my face

I left my culture and wisdom's learned behind
But I will carry the importance of your limited time

I'm out in the open and life seems dull
Oh, how I wish I hadn't quit school … it wasn't as boring as I thought it was

Peace

No one is going to make it unless together we try
We yell out for freedom, but for peace we give a small cry

Our boys are home because of peace between two nations, you know
But how many of our boys called it freedom when they refused to go

Hundreds and thousands gave their lives some don't even know why
Yet we contradict the men who held their guns high

Has our society given up hope for hope long sought in the past
Or will we stand together for peace with our fellow man at last?

Brothers and sisters of America, it is up to you and me
To make this world a better place and to live in harmony

People Are Different

I have met people of all nationalities and races
many are the same, only with different faces

Some are rich, some are poor, others in between
some were kind, some were blind, others I wish I'd never seen

People can be strange, some with lives they tend to waste
but for me, life is a gift, and I feel the giver had good taste

I've met people who think of the past and foresee the future
I've met others who live in the present and remain unsure

If everyone would try to understand
Then no one would make uncertain demands

Sometimes we do what we have to do
And yet there are many who do what they want too

There are those who think of the feelings of others
While there are those that forget that we're sisters and brothers

People are like things, they too can fall apart
They may act as though they're bad and yet be good at heart

Some people are content only every once in awhile
But then there are those that always appear to smile

Some people really care about the things that they say
The world is a better place in which to live if we all care in some way

Viking Team

They're running across the field and they're wearing a smile
The coach told them, "Win, or you'll run 10 miles!"

The Vikings know they'll win this game
They'll not walk away with their heads hung in shame

The game has started and the team is doing grand
They make one last touchdown and shake their opponents' hands

The Vikings are a team and that's the way they play
There aren't many opponents that win against their team spirit on display

An Outstanding Personality

When I look at the beauty of this world in my mind
I think of the things that make it shine

The same shine that individual personalities show
Their smiles, their walks, the patterns of life they follow

An outstanding personality is one that is seldom overlooked
As it stands out like a marked page in a black book

There are times when you feel lonesome and neglected too
And yet you continue to smile, for there is little more you can do

It's That Time Again

It comes a few times a year
It's when things seem to change and bring about tears

Your brain is overworked and gradually you lose control
And when it finally stops, your mind feels overworked, bereft, and cold

You're watching and waiting as time seems to fly
But uneasiness is still there and it will not pass you by

You have a feeling that you want to run and try to get away
But something holds you back, making sure that you stay

Yes, it's that time again, the one that comes during the school year
The time when you're scared to death because … "Exams are here."

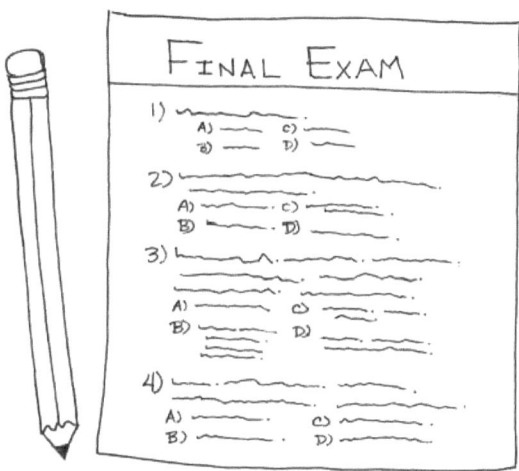

A Sudden Change in Life

A sudden change in life creates things that are difficult to speak of
... when they are, we must ascertain the difference between hate and love

The words of love, the way we live, the way we care, the way we feel, and
    the way we act
The pains of love, the way we fight, the way we yell, and the way we change the facts

As painful information is forthcoming, a sudden change in life comes about
making our feelings easier to hurt when someone raises a voice or shouts

There are days when you just want to run and hide
There are days when your future looks bright and you beam with pride

Life is a mystery and yet you refuse to give up and leave
You cherish every moment of joy, happiness, and times you feel free

Love and hate in life bring about sudden, day-to-day change
as reactions from the ones you love grow more and more strange

You see sudden changes in life, as they will always unfold
You live through hurt and pain while holding close the joys as you grow old

Drawing Designs

I drew a pig that looked like a duck
My teacher gave me a grade, which was my good luck

I drew a horse and felt proud of myself
It had a hen on it's back that needed some help

My drawing isn't good enough to compare to others' art
I guess I'm not an artist, but I've been told I have book smarts

Drawing designs or preparing a sketch are not something of interest
But I want a better grade in art class so that my report card will impress

I have come to accept that with my artwork, you'd need a critical eye
It isn't for the weak of heart and will make you either laugh or cry

4-H

4-H is for four hearts that left me in great pain
The ones I've experienced are my greatest shame

Have you ever thought you were in love and found it wasn't wise
My heart has been broken four times and each was of a different size

H.B.L. and I never had very much in common from the start
He flirted with other girls, ignoring me and breaking my heart

G.E.T. was very handsome but I realized that was all
He acted more like a brother to me than a guy to call

R.S. was in my life for a few months, but I'll not soon forget about that
I fell head-over-heels in love with the long-legged rat

K.M.J. was quite a catch but I never really caught the fake
It was nice to put him out of my mind with my heart at stake

Many girls I've heard have heartbreaks galore, so much more than mine
The 4-H I lived through are reminders of love lost in another time

I Thank You

I thank you for being one of the forwards in my life
You've helped me to make it through many of my greatest strifes

You were there when I was a freshman, sophomore, and junior in high school
I know that you will be the one for me to thank as a senior too

You are one of the stronger backups for the student body
You have several jobs to look after, but your work is never tardy

You've helped me make it through some of my worst trials
It wasn't so much the school work as the students with their words so vile

There were times when I felt like I wanted to give up as a whole
 You were there to encourage me and to remind me to stay strong and bold

Mrs. Silliman, I never would've made it my four years at Central without your help
It was your words of wisdom and support that guided me through my every step

Sometimes I would falter and start to turn away
Then I'd think of the opportunities I wanted in life and I was determined to stay

GTO

The GTO was ready to go
Revving its engine and keeping the throttle down low

The car was fast and anxious to get on the track
When the driver said, "Baby, you're getting a flat"

The driver stopped the car and began to look with an eye for detail
He didn't like what he saw as he touched the big nail

The tire was going flat and the spare didn't fit
He had to get off the track so that he wouldn't get hit

He didn't want to be late and he knew things would soon start
He called up his friends, who brought a tire and spare parts

He made it back to the race track just in time
The GTO was holding up fine

He was about to lose the race with mud on his face
When his GTO passed the other cars by as he came in first place!

My Living Angel

One morning I got up to hear a bell ringing
Sitting on my doorstep was a little bird singing

As I opened my door to let him in
I asked what he was singing and where he'd been

He said, mother nor father had he to be near
There is no one around when he gets hurt, to shed a tear

I opened my heart to my new little friend
We did everything together until the very end

I woke up one night to find that he was gone ... to my sorrow
He'd left me a note saying he'd remember me through his forever tomorrow's

My Living Angel, I'll always believe,
was that tiny bird who was there during my time of need

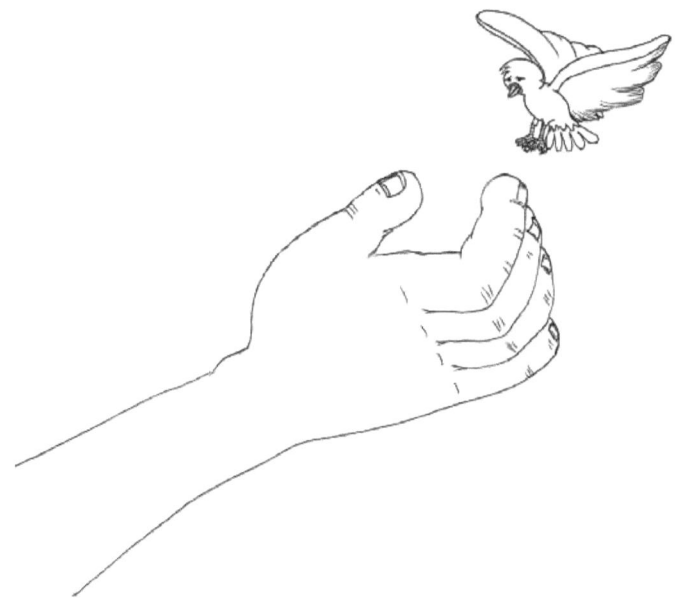

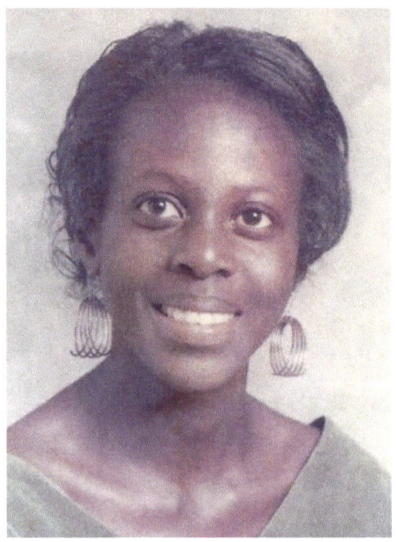

About the Author

Writing began as a form of escape for me from the world of reality, allowing for self-expression while I lived in a foster home with my siblings and many other children. Some of the poems were written without thought, while others were written as a form of communication without the element of verbal interaction. The poems weren't always about anything or anyone specific.

I grew up learning and believing that children weren't always meant to be seen or heard, so I learned to be creative in my invisibility while hiding in plain sight. My poetry allowed me an "out" in order to somehow feel connected to something during frequent periods of aloneness.

I have lived in Alaska with my beautiful family for over 27 years. I have a husband of over 40 years and together we have, among our extended family, six beautiful adult children and six grandchildren.

www.ingramcontent.com/pod-product-compliance
Lightning Source LLC
Chambersburg PA
CBHW040059160426
43193CB00002B/19